TWENTY-ONE DAYS OF REIKI

by
Adam Sartwell

COPPER
CAULDRON
PUBLISHING

Credits

Writing: Adam Sartwell

Editing: Matooka Moonbear, Tina Whittle

Layout & Publishing: Steve Kenson

For more information visit:
www.coppercauldronpublishing.com

ISBN 978-1-940755-04-5, Second Revised Printing

Printed in the U.S.A.

Table of Contents

Introduction

When I first learned Reiki, my teacher suggested that after we had attuned, we should do self Reiki every day for 21 days. She called it a Reiki cleanse. It was based on the 21 days that Doctor Usui spent on the sacred mountain asking for aid in learning the laying-on of hands. She said it was both a great way to get your positions for self Reiki down and to help clean out your own energy bodies so you could be a clearer channel of Reiki energy. I have since learned that not everyone who has had Reiki training was asked to do this, and I thought it would be a good idea to share it. I found it so helpful that I do it as a rite of discipline every couple of years to aid me in my own healing process. Though it was not required by my teacher, I did the same cleanse for Reiki One, Two, and Master Teacher.

I was so inspired by my involvement with the #13daysofmagic project by Devin Hunter that I thought it would be good to set myself a goal and do more short-term blogs with a focus. The idea of doing 21 days of Reiki came to me as a great way to both do some self healing and share some wisdom—I have collected those writings into this book, and I invite you to join me on this journey of healing.

My own Reiki cleanse starts on the 1st of December and ends on the 21st. The Winter Solstice is a great time of new beginnings when the light of the world in the Northern Hemisphere begins to return. I have timed the ending of the cleanse for that time, so that as our energy clears, we can being a new cycle of the year. You can join me in this healing work at any level of Reiki attunement by doing a daily self-healing. The work is most appropriate for those who have Reiki Two or higher. That being said, if there is a way for those who have attained Reiki One to work with the material, I offer an adapted form.

Some suggestions for those joining me on this Reiki cleanse:

- Set time in your schedule every day for doing self Reiki.
- Get some music to listen to that will help you relax during your session.
- Don't do your session in bed. If you are like me, you will fall asleep!
- If you are in a rush, do distance Reiki on yourself, but don't do it too often because you will be missing the point. (Sorry, Reiki Ones, no time cheats for you.)
- Tell your support network that you are doing this work, and warn them that it may bring up issues. Friends, family, and your therapist may wonder what is going on unless you've clued them in beforehand.
- Be gentle with yourself during these 21 days. You will find that you are more sensitive to media, so consider avoiding anything with graphic violence or online discussions that get you heated and upset.
- Drink lots of water! When you are doing this cleanse, it will aid you in flushing emotional and physical toxins.

- Take a Epsom salt water bath or do a salt scrub to help you cleanse and clear.
- Set a healing intention for your cleanse. For example: "My healing cleanse supports my work to love and nurture myself more" or "My Reiki cleanse brings me closer to my ideal weight."
- Reward yourself with something fun every week of the cleanse.

Each day of the Reiki cleanse will cover a different topic. You can add the teaching or exercise to your practice if you want, and I encourage you to do so. The only requirement is that you do a full self healing every day. I hope you will join me on this journey.

Reiki & Affirmations

We are constantly co-creating with the universe whether we realize this or not. Our subconscious mind communicates with our higher self, telling it what we want by what we focus on each day. Our conscious mind chooses the focus, and in doing so, programs the subconscious. One of the New Age ways of working with this ability to co-create is to use affirmations to reprogram our mind to attract different circumstances. Affirmations are short positive sentences that affirm the changes you want to make in your life.

To create an affirmation, you should follow some simple rules. Affirmations are always formed in the most positive way possible. "I am not late" is less effective than "I am always on time." The only time a negative phrasing should be used is to release old patterns of behavior, and even then, it should be followed by a new positive affirmation. For example, "I am no longer wasting my time," followed by "I now use my time to the fullest in the most fulfilling ways."

Affirmations create something new. If you are just trying to change what is, you will be in resistance to things you have already created. When you are speaking the affirmation, you are affirming something on the subjective plane of awareness. Once you have created it there, you can then create it in your life. When you use an affirmation, you are creating new ways of being instead of struggling to re-create past experiences.

Affirmations always affirm the present tense. The thing you want to happen has already happened on the subjective level. You have to give it energy so that it will manifest in the now you are in. If you put your affirmation in the future, it will always stay in your future and never be in your present!

Affirmations need to be short. If your affirmation gets too long, it will lose its effectiveness. Focus on what you really want and concentrate on the rest another time. Some people put too many intentions into their affirmations.

You must believe your affirmation could be true and it should take into account your feelings on the matter. You can say, "I am a sexy underwear model" until you're blue in the face, but if you don't believe you could ever be an underwear model, you're not going to get very far. Instead say, "I am radiantly attractive and healthy." Which is a bit more believable. Because if you don't believe it, your subconscious won't either.

Affirmations are not there to change our feelings. Our feelings are important and have a lot to teach us. By accepting them and expressing them in a healthy way, we can then get to the root of their meaning. You can use affirmations to change your circumstances, so the root of the problem is not there anymore.

Once you have created your affirmation for something you want in your life, it is time to start programing for it. Take time to get relaxed by releasing any tension in your body. Imagine a wave of healing energy flowing through your body, helping you relax muscle by muscle. When all is relaxed, draw the emotional-mental symbol on the screen of your mind and say its name three times. This fades, and you then visualize what your affirmation's intention is as if it were already happening. For example, if your affirmation is "I am radiantly healthy; all my choices are healthy ones," you could visualize yourself healthy and happy. Really feel what it would be like to have your goal. Use your senses and your emotions to really get into it. Then affirm your goal with your affirmation: "I am radiantly healthy and all my choices are healthy ones." Draw the emotional-mental symbol again to imprint this goal on your subconscious. Come out of your meditative state and then ground by doing something physical to give your subconscious time to do its magick.

Affirmations are best when they are repeated in this meditative way multiple times. It could take up to a month. Once you have worked on the same thing for a month, stop doing that visualization and affirmation. Work on something else for a while to give the universe time to work on it. You may have moments where negative thinking towards your goal arises during the day. First recognize that this was former programing, then say "I neutralize that" or "I cancel that program." You can then use the Raku symbol to end the habit of that programing. The Raku symbol is like a lightning bolt. If you don't feel comfortable with that, use an X to cross it out. Immediately after say the affirmation, you are working within a positive attitude.

Reiki for Food & Water

We live in a world of form. We have to nurture our bodies and make sure that they have what they need. One of the things we need most is water. Some metaphysical free-thinkers suggest that low water intake can make aches and pains worse, lead to depression, and increase stress. Physically it can lead to headaches and worse. Your ability to process psychic information may also be reduced. One of the tricks of the old spiritualist mediums was to drink more water before they did psychic work to give them a clearer transmission from the other side.

Since we have to take in water to survive on this planet, why not just charge that water for your highest good with some Reiki? Grab your water bottle or cup and place your hands around it, letting the Reiki flow into the water. You can also say a prayer of intent to add a focus to the energy, something like: "I charge this water with Reiki for my highest healing good, to heal me on all levels and to help me flush out of my system any toxins or toxic energy." Hold the water until you feel the Reiki has done its job and has ceased to flow. It doesn't hurt to add a visualization of the water being filled with radiant light, perhaps a colored light matching your intention.

In the Feri tradition and some Huna-based traditions, they practice a rite called Kala. Participants visualize tensions and energetic blocks or thought forms called complexes flowing into the water, then visualize bringing more energy into the water than the complexes and tensions can handle, thus dissolving them in the water's new energy. They then drink the changed water to reclaim the power and energy they just transformed. This can be done with Reiki as well.

Take a few deep breaths, becoming aware of your body. Search your body for any packet of stress, tension, or emotion that it is storing. Imagine gently pushing any of these out your hands. I usually see them as blobs of energy. They flow out into your cup of water. Now concentrate on giving the glass Reiki until you sense that the things you released are healed and dissolved. Drink the water to reabsorb the energy that was just transformed. This is a great way to purify yourself.

Your food can also be blessed with Reiki energy. This only takes a few moments before you start to eat. You can draw the Reiki symbols over your food or just hold your hands over your food allowing the Reiki to flow for a few moments. I like to say a little intention statement: "I charge this meal with Reiki for my highest healing good. May what I need from it be absorbed and all that is not for my highest good just pass through me. As I Reiki it, I send Reiki to that which gave up its life so that I might live in blessing. So mote it be!"

Blessing your food and water is a great practice to help you heal. It also brings attention to what you are eating and whether or not you feel it is truly for your highest good.

Reiki Baths

The root of any disease or discomfort we experience on the physical level starts as a blockage or thought-form—a dis-ease—in our energy body. Around each of us is an aura containing our spiritual, mental, and emotional selves, our blueprint, and our physical body. When we Reiki ourselves, we fill our energy body with Reiki's universal energy. As we heal, our energy body uses the Reiki to push blockages or thought-forms out of the system. This is why sometimes the body will suddenly change reactions to a disease when Reiki is used. That sore neck of yours could become a release for your feelings of being overwhelmed, first transforming into the thoughts that make up that feeling and then releasing into spirit, leaving you with the lesson to not be so attached to the outcome that you waste all your time worrying.

My first Reiki teacher would say that as we healed with Reiki, the complex or block that created the problem would move outward from our physical into the emotional, mental, and then spiritual body. To help it release, she suggested a bath in traditionally cleansing additives. Bathing for spiritual cleansing is a part of many traditions. Some even have baths designed to bring about certain manifestations. I would like to share the ones she taught me that I have personally found very cleansing.

One simple bath is to put a handful of Epsom salts in the bathwater after it has been charged with Reiki for cleansing and healing. Not only are Epsom salts energetically cleansing, they are also helpful for aches and pains. To use this technique in the shower, you can make a cleansing salt scrub with Epsom salts and a little olive oil (just avoid applying to any sensitive areas). Epsom salts can also be used in a foot bath for an ingrown toenail. I will sometimes add a little Reiki-charged sea salt and some baking soda, a combination that gives the water a great feel. It can be pretty drying to the skin, however, so drink lots of water and moisturize!

The other way my teacher suggested creating a healing bath is to use a cup of apple cider vinegar in the bathwater. My mom used to say you could use apple cider vinegar "to clean a brick." This is true on the spiritual level as well as the physical. An apple cider vinegar bath has a pleasant feeling on the skin and helps you get spiritually clean as well. You can combine the Epsom salts with it, but that isn't necessary.

I've picked up a few other spiritually cleansing baths over the years. Hyssop is mentioned in the Bible and other traditions as having the ability to make you "as pure as snow." Put a tablespoon in about three cups of boiling water and let it steep for a couple of minutes. Strain the liquid from the herb and pour it into your bathwater. Hyssop is said to help those who feel guilty, to bring forgiveness, and to make you spiritually cleansed.

Another way to help you cleanse is to put a little Florida water into the bath. This perfume, well known for its citrus and floral scents, has been used by multiple traditions to cleanse and bless. You can get the manufactured one in a botanica or order it online. I like to make my own. There are many different recipes and ways to make it.

The most important part of doing any of these spiritual cleansing baths is to Reiki charge the ingredients and set your intention to aid you to clear and cleanse yourself. I like to draw the symbols for empowerment, emotional healing, and distant healing over the bath. Then I say something like, "I charge this bath to cleanse me on all levels of anything harmful and fill its place with healing universal energy for my highest healing good." Then I get in and relax and let the stress of the day just wash away!

Reiki Containers

One of the best ways of manifesting and healing with the power of distance Reiki is to use a Reiki box or Reiki bowl. I first learned this technique from Christopher Penczak's book *The Magick of Reiki*. It is a great book if you are looking for ways to enhance your Reiki practice. (I may be a little biased though, as Christopher is one of my partners.) A Reiki box or bowl is a consecrated vessel holding written petitions and then given Reiki daily to have these petitions for healing manifest. This is a practice I incorporate into my daily devotionals so I can help myself and others.

To make a Reiki box or bowl, you first have to make or obtain a box or bowl. I made a box because then I could travel with it without losing the petition slips. If you have a more stationary lifestyle, a bowl may be more reasonable for you—we use a bowl for healing petitions on the Temple's healing altar, for example. Once you have obtained your vessel, cleanse it with some incense, homemade holy water, visualizations of the violet flame, or you can Reiki it three times, first with the empowerment symbol, next with the emotional symbol, and then finally with the empowerment symbol again. After it has been cleansed, say an intention while charging it with Reiki. Something like:

"I charge and consecrate this Reiki (box or bowl) to aid me in focusing the power of my Reiki to manifest changes, to bring healing, and to catalyze my will. All petitions for healing and lists within this bowl will manifest for the highest healing good of all concerned, harming none. So mote it be!"

After you have done this consecration ritual, put in your first petition and start using the vessel right away. Petitions are pieces of paper where an intention or prayer is placed. You can use any kind of paper that speaks to you. I know traditions that use only the brown paper from a brown paper bag; others use parchment paper. I use any paper I have on hand. The petition can be long or short depending on your preferences. For healing I usually use a very short version of the following:

"In the name of the Goddess and God, by the healing flow of Reiki, may Anybody McHealme be healed of their affliction and made healthy and whole for the highest healing good of all concerned, harming none. So mote it be!"

Before performing a healing with the bowl, you should also get permission from the person in need. Not everyone likes Reiki sent to them. For a manifestation, you may want something a little more detailed on your petition, something like:

" I, Adam Sartwell, call upon the Goddess, God, and the Great Spirit, to manifest a pair of roller skates with Hello Kitty on them in size ten-and-a-half men's. May the healing power of Reiki manifest this for me before the next full moon. I ask that this be for the highest good, harming none. So mote it be!"

Every day, Reiki the bowl or box using the distance symbol. If you are a Reiki One, just Reiki charge the box. You can put as many petitions as you can fit in your box. There are many sites that have a healing list of names of those in need of healing—the Temple of Witchcraft has such a list that changes every new moon. This is a perfect thing to put in your healing box or bowl. I like to have one day of the month where I gather up all the petitions and burn them to release the healing. My own practice matches the Temple of Witchcraft's healing list cycle. You may feel more comfortable doing it on full moons or twice a moon cycle at the full and new moons to connect to the waxing and waning energies of the moon. It is up to you.

I was inspired about two years ago by the novel *The Help* to begin to write my prayers, like one of the women in the book does. I have a deep love of little Moleskine journals, so I dedicated one as a blessing book using a similar consecration as the one I just mentioned. In my blessing book, I wrote out prayers like the petitions for healing and manifesting. I also wrote out prayers of thanks to the gods for the manifestations and blessings in my life. Every workday, I would Reiki the book on my lap as I drove into work. When I got to work early, I would write one prayer of thanks for something I was grateful for. Sometimes I would only have time to Reiki the book. I recently went through the book ripping out pages of things that had manifested or healed and all pages with prayers of gratitude on them to burn at my next healing ritual. I couldn't believe how many of those prayers had come true. My book is now a lot slimmer!

Whether you use a box, a bowl, or a blessing book, it can help you create a simple and rewarding daily spiritual practice.

The Reiki Healing Poppet

Reiki has multiple ways of sending healing at a distance. Out of those ways, one resonates strongly with me when people have a long-term disease: a healing poppet. Perhaps it is because I learned to do healing with a poppet before I learned about Reiki, but I have found this method powerful. A poppet is a handmade doll representing a single person in a healing ritual. It is akin to a "doll baby" or "voodoo doll." I use this healing method only for family and dear friends because it is time consuming, but it is effective. The work that I have done with these poppets extended and improved the lives of my father, my grandmothers, and my partner's mother. It is not a fix-all, however—when it is time, it is time. Sometimes that highest healing good is passing over to the other side.

To make a Reiki poppet, you need a drawing of a vaguely human shape for a pattern, some white cloth, scissors, white thread, a fabric marker or other permanent marker, a tag lock (more information forthcoming), healing herbs, a healing crystal such as quartz or rose quartz, some stuffing, and some holy water. Use your pattern to cut out two sides of the poppet. Sew the poppet's sides together, leaving a little room (usually at the head) for stuffing.

Gather your herbs to stuff the poppet. Use herbs that are appropriate for the affliction your subject has. Any good herbal remedy book or an Internet search for herbs good for the healing diseases will turn up some ideas. If you don't know the affliction, use some general magickal healing herbs: cinquefoil, comfrey, coriander, fennel, echinacea, lavender, lemon balm, rosemary, rue, sage, or St. John's wort are good choices. Use a combination of three, seven, or nine herbs. Mix the herbs together, giving them Reiki to bring out their natural healing magick.

Stuff the poppet with the stuffing and herbs until you get to the chest. At the chest, you will add your tag lock. A tag lock is something linked to the person that can give you a better connection to them. It could be a piece of hair, a fingernail clipping, a picture of them, a ring they wear, something they have signed, or if you can't get any of these things, their full name and astrological Sun sign. If you have their astrological information, you could also put in their chart.

In the chest near the left side of the doll, put the healing crystal. Before you put it in, charge the crystal with Reiki, imprinting it with the intention of bringing this person healing for their highest healing good. Stuff the rest of the doll with stuffing and herbs. Use a pencil to pack it into all the nooks and crannies of the doll. When you have it good and stuffed sew the hole in the head closed. Use your marker to put a smiling face on the poppet and draw a heart on the left side of the chest. Inside the heart, put the zodiac symbol of the person's sun sign. Write their full name down the leg or on the chest of the doll.

With your holy water anoint the doll, saying:

"By the infinite source, from which all Reiki flows, I consecrate this poppet to be (full name of person). All healing Reiki that is given to this poppet is given to (full name) for their highest healing good. Any excess or unneeded Reiki flows into the environment around them, healing it for its highest healing good. This poppet is charged to only do the highest healing good and may harm none. Heart to heart, they are one, only bound until the healing is done! So mote it be!"

Reiki the poppet immediately after. When I made these poppets, I would Reiki them on a regular schedule depending on how desperate the need was. For some, it was every day, and for others, once a week. I let my intuition be my guide. I recommend adding breaks into whatever you choose to do as your Reiki schedule. This gives the person who is receiving the treatment time to both let it work on them and to rest. You don't want to bring up so many things to heal and work through that it overwhelms the subject. This is why the intention statement above says that any excess or unneeded Reiki will flow into the environment around them, so that you don't overload them. I feel it is better to give them your full attention during the worst of the illness and Reiki the poppet directly, but once they begin to feel better, you can put the poppet into your Reiki bowl or box.

When they have fully recovered and you want to dismantle the poppet, get a knife or athame, your stitch ripper, and the poppet. Pass the knife around the poppet three times front to back and three times down the sides, symbolically cutting the ties between it and the person. Then say:

"By the infinite source, from which all Reiki flows, I sever all ties to this poppet and (full name of person) for the highest healing good. From heart to heart, healing was done, no longer bound, they are two, not one."

Use your seam ripper to open a hole in the poppet and begin to remove the stuffing and herbs. When you get to the heart, take out the tag lock and the crystal. Dispose of the tag lock. Cleanse the crystal. Take the stuffing and herbs and give them back to nature by burning or burying them. You can burn or bury the rest of the poppet.

This healing method is powerful and should not be taken lightly.

Honoring Reiki Ancestors

One of the things that I have done for years is honor my ancestors and those who have guided the magickal systems I have learned. My ancestor altar is a place where I honor and commune with my ancestors. I find that doing offerings to them helps me communicate with them and get their help on any issue. It also gives me a chance to offer gratitude for all that I have because of these people. You can also honor your Reiki line with a simple ritual at an altar, creating a greater connection to the masters of Reiki beyond the veil. You may find that if you make this a part of your practice, you can receive guidance when doing Reiki or healing work.

If you have been attuned to Reiki, you should get a list from your teacher that details your line of Reiki back to Dr. Usui. If you haven't, you might want to do a little research on the Reiki Masters of the past. You could also start with Dr. Makao Usui, Dr. Chujiro Hayashi, and Hawayo Takata. Dr. Usui started the system of Reiki. Dr. Hayashi added the hand positions to Reiki. Takata brought Reiki to the world. Once you have a list of your Reiki lineage, write it out on a nice piece of paper (perhaps even framing it). Find a place for you to honor your lineage, like a small altar. I use our ancestor altar because they are my ancestors of Reiki. Instead of a list, you may want to obtain pictures of some of the people of your lineage. This gives you a focus for your energy.

Make a space to honor them. Set it up with their pictures and your list of lineage. Burn some incense to honor them. Light a candle to give them energy. Get a glass of water to put in the space. Charge the water with Reiki and write in the air the Reiki symbols, especially the distance symbol. Say a prayer such as this one:

"There is one power that is the universal light of Reiki. I honor those who have carried this line forward to me. I send Reiki through time to thank them for their work both in this world and in the one beyond. I ask that they be at peace and find spiritual enlightenment beyond the veil. May this candle light their way. May this Reiki empower them to aid us from beyond the veil. May this incense give them the breath to speak. May the waters of life aid their healing work. So mote it be."

Take some time to just be silent after you have said this prayer before your altar. In this silence, you may get feelings, words, pictures in your head, or a sudden idea. Know that this is how those beyond the veil communicate with us. I like to refresh my offerings once a week. I usually do it on Saturday because it is ruled by Saturn, which I associate with the dead.

If you are going to do a healing session, you may want to call to them to be with you during the session. I will say a short prayer before my client arrives asking them to guide and aid me in this healing. Depending on the client and my own whims, I may burn incense, light a candle, and refresh the glass of water on the ancestor altar before a session. I will sometimes feel other hands with my hands as I do the healing work. This is a sign that they are with me.

Clearing with Candle Meditation

A meditation I learned from *Reiki, a Way of Life* by Patricia Rose Upczak has stuck with me through the years. It is a simple way to help clear away any energies that are not for our highest good. I do this meditation if I feel blocked or stuck in some way. It is straightforward, but as a Witch, I add things to it to make it even more effective.

To do this practice, you need a candle of whatever color you choose. I use colors with cleansing and clearing properties, but you can use white, which is an all-purpose color. You can use purple to bring in the power of transformation and the violet flame. If you need some powerful cleansing, use a black candle to absorb and banish.

After choosing my candle, I anoint it with a cleansing oil like van van, altar oil, or a citrus oil like orange or lemon. Then, to make the energy extra strong, I put the candle in a bowl of salt water. Salt water has unique cleansing properties—it is the basic composition of holy water. Reiki the salt water to enhance its abilities to clear and cleanse. Reiki charge the candle for the same intention and place it in the bowl of salt water. Light the candle and get comfortable.

Take some deep breaths and imagine healing waves of energy relaxing your muscles from the top of your head to the bottom of your feet. Bring your hands up over your head and sweep them down the length of your body and out toward the candle and bowl. Visualize any packets of unhealthy energy flowing with your hands towards the candle to be cleansed. Do about nine of these sweeps of the unwanted energies in your aura. After you have done the sweeps, gaze at the candle's flame. With each breath you release any complexes, thoughts, or energies you wish to cleanse yourself of. This is also a great way to cleanse your heart and mind when you're upset or getting ready for bed.

When you feel clear, give yourself a Reiki session to fill any spaces that have been cleared with renewed energy. When you are done, do nine more sweeps to stabilize your energy. You can let the candle burn down or snuff it and use it for a couple of days' worth of cleansing meditation. After you have done this meditation, you may want to take a break before you do another cleansing just to let your energies settle.

Healing the Inner Child

No childhood is perfect. We all have things we go through growing up that shape the people we become. As adults we have moments where those childhood experiences come into play again. Trauma like abuse, neglect, prejudice, and loss can cripple our abilities to be fully functioning adults. That child still lives within us in our psyche. The child who didn't feel loved, the child who lived in fear, the child who lost innocence: they still exist within. They yearn to be loved, soothed, and made safe.

Adults who go through traumas as children often turn to coping strategies that make them feel they are getting what that child needs. Sex and food to feel love, isolation to feel safe, bravado and sarcasm to hide their pain. There are those who seek drugs and other addictions to numb the feelings coming from this hurt child. Thankfully there are good choices to be made to help deal with this: therapy, art, music, poetry, meditation, ritual, and getting to the core of that need. Another way to begin to heal ourselves is through Reiki. We are holistic beings that exist on multiple levels, so it may take more than one method to help heal and empower. Reiki is only one way to heal and should be used in combination with other treatments.

Healing the child self with Reiki is easiest at for those who have at least Reiki Two attunement. Reiki Ones begin to heal themselves by doing Reiki treatments on themselves.

Reiki Twos and above have the distance symbol to aid them in healing. The distance symbol connects to the spirit realm where there is no time and no space, because they are all one time and one space. With the distance symbol, we can heal ourselves in the past as well as the future. My favorite way to heal the child within is to get my favorite teddy bear from when I was a kid to use as a surrogate in a distance healing. The bear holds memories of my younger self and aids me in connecting to this time. It isn't necessary for you to use an old stuffed animal or toy, but it does aid the working.

This healing method takes time. You may start healing the younger self and have more issues and memories come to the foreground of your mind. Let them come, be aware of them, and then let them go so you can go back to the healing you set out to do. After the healing, write down in your journal what came up. Was there something else that you feel also needs healing? In your next healing session, send Reiki to that moment or issue. Healing is like peeling back the layers of an onion—heal one thing and something else arises. Doing the healing is so much more healthy than ignoring the problem, however. This technique can aid you in healing past issues, but it won't erase what was done in the past. It will affect how it works itself out in your present.

For your beginning session, get your surrogate or visualize your child self between your hands. Chant and visualize the distance symbol. Set your intention to heal your inner child. Follow up with the empowerment symbol and emotional symbol. I like to visualize and chant them in my head while I am doing the distance healing. Let the Reiki flow. Be aware of anything that comes up for you from your childhood and then let it go. You can write these down later. Continue to Reiki your child self until you feel the healing is done. This can be five minutes to half an hour. When done, remove your hands and clap three times, ending the flow. I like to draw Ra Ku to distance myself from the work for objectivity. Journal any feelings, memories, or issues that came up. You may also like to journal about how the healing felt and how you feel afterward.

In your next session, decide on one of the feelings, memories, or issues that came up and set your intention to heal that one issue. Reiki that is focused on one issue instead of a broad topic or goal sees a greater effect in healing because it is less diffuse. Remember you are healing, and give yourself time and space to just be. After doing this work, you might need small breaks between sessions; you might also need to seek out assistance and support. As long as you continue the work, the breaks between sessions can be just as healing.

"Reiki the Situation"

My partner Christopher had just come back from Chicago where he had been teaching all weekend. He was telling us about Rosina's Reiki for Kids class and how little kids at the event would repeat Rosina's instructions, saying "Reiki the situation" in her accent and inflection. It was so super cute that for weeks afterward it became our catch phrase to each other. Troubles at work, students gone wild, disturbing politics, fights with friends, and more got the response "Reiki the situation" in a little kid voice. Even though we sometimes were just having a laugh, the power of this one statement stayed with me.

Reiki is guided to the highest healing good. This makes it perfect to use to heal situations in our lives. After you have given a situation Reiki, it will come to a conclusion that was for the highest good. To enhance this effect, you could also call out to the higher selves of all the people involved, including your own, to create the highest healing good in this situation. Then send the Reiki using a distance healing method. I am not saying this will end a problem and you will always be happy with the result. The highest healing good doesn't always align with our personal goals, but will always align with the higher will of our higher selves. Our higher selves are always trying to lead us to do what we came to learn and do in this world.

I had a friend from college (living far away from me at the time) who started to fight with me through email about how I should have supported her in her time of need. She had thought that I would have psychically picked up on her needs and helped her. We had multiple emails that just kept getting worse. I started to Reiki the situation because I felt like there was nothing I could do to make this right between us. After a couple days of this, I received a message from her that I needed to stop emailing with her and delete anything she'd sent me. Though my personal goal was to keep a friendship that had been so good in the past, my higher will said it was time to move on because it was getting toxic. I believe I got this message because I "Reiki'ed the situation."

I have used this healing method on multiple situations: work situations, romantic situations, friendships, holiday gift shopping, and many more. More often than not, it worked in the favor of all involved and made the situation more healthy. Just be aware that this technique can cause what is called a healing crisis, which is an issue that is brought up by doing healing. It happens so that we can work through it to get to the root issue and learn its lesson. A healing crisis can sometimes get worse before it gets better, but there is always a moment of clarity that illuminates the underlying issues or the lesson. After that moment of clarity, the situation changes rapidly.

Healing Inheritance Patterns

Our family teaches us about life when we are growing. Our DNA comes from them. We are intrinsically linked to them through our blood and education and through our family karma. Our link to our family passes habits both good and bad: diseases, complexes, patterns, abilities, memories, and sometimes the karma of our ancestors. All of these patterns can be changed and improved.

One Native teaching is that anything you do in your life, including healing, affects seven generations. Some believe this goes both forward and backward down the ancestral line. So just by starting to heal yourself, you have begun the practice of healing your family, ancestors, and your descendants. Your healing of yourself ripples throughout time and can aid all of us. It is much like the Hermetic principle of "as above, so below." When we heal what is inside of us, we heal our microcosm, which is then reflected out in the macrocosm. Here you thought that you were just healing yourself and now you are adding to the healing of the world!

The things we can inherit from our family and ancestral line create what I like to call an inheritance pattern. It is a pattern of being that seems to infect multiple members of a family. This can be a physical inheritance pattern such as diabetes or hair loss. Emotional patterns like stubbornness to new ideas or indecisiveness when given a choice can manifest this way too, as can relational patterns like how you interact with a spouse or with prosperity. Mental patterns are a part of it too, such as thoughts about traditions or always wanting to please those you love because they could leave. Lastly there are also spiritual patterns, like a tendency to be dogmatic or doubt intuition. I am sure there are many more categories I could give you, but the important thing to understand is that there is an energetic pattern that you and your family members enact. Most of these patterns served a purpose at some point, and because they made such a strong imprint, they are passed on.

When I was a kid, a friend of my mom told a story about how every Christmas they would cut the ends off the ham before they put it in the roaster. One Christmas she said to her sister, "Do you know why we cut this part of the ham off?" The sister then replied that it was the way that their mother had always done it. So they called their mother and asked her why she always cut off the ends of the ham. She didn't know why either, and said that her mother had always done that too. So she called up their grandmother and asked why she would cut off the ends of the ham. Her answer was that she didn't have a large enough roasting pan, and it wouldn't have fit otherwise. The sisters and mother had been wasting ham for years because of this inheritance pattern they had. Once they knew it was folly, they changed the pattern. I know this is not an extreme example, but it reveals how and why such patterns can start.

I like to do work with inheritance patterns during the waning moon to tap into its abilities to banish and diminish, though you can do this work at any time you need. During the waxing moon, a time of growth and manifestation, I introduce a new pattern to fill the old pattern's place, one that is more in line with how I choose to live my life.

Though you can do this fully through visualization, I like to make a petition or list of inheritance patterns I would like to remove. This will focus my healing work, making it easier to transform these patterns into usable energies. An example of a petition would be:

"I, Adam Sartwell, call upon the Infinite Great Spirit from which all Reiki emanates to remove, banish, and dissipate the pattern of stress eating from myself, and if they are willing, from the seven generations forward and back for the highest healing good, harming none. So mote it be!"

A list would be more like:

"I, Adam Sartwell, call upon the Infinite Great Spirit from which all Reiki emanates to remove, banish and dissipate the following patterns:

I banish the inheritance pattern of stress eating

I banish the inheritance pattern of wasting ham.

I banish the inheritance pattern of indecisiveness

May these be healed both within me and moving outward to my seven generations forward and back, if they are willing, for the highest good, harming none. So mote it be!"

This petition can be put in your box, book, or bowl for Reiki, or you can do a special distance Reiki just on the slip of paper. You could read it out loud three times every time you Reiki it, or you could read it three times the first time and fold it so you can't see it and Reiki it for the rest of the moon cycle. I find the latter method works better for me because it gives my subconscious room to work on it. Burn the paper when your moon cycle has ended. Then make a list of positive patterns you would like to adopt to replace these things. Something like:

"I, Adam Sartwell, call upon the Infinite Great Spirit from which all Reiki emanates to co-create with me these healthy patterns:

I embrace the new pattern of meditation when I feel it is needed.

I enjoy using all parts of the ham and thank the spirit of the pig for feeding me.

My heart and mind are one, making it easy to decide effectively.

May these healthy patterns or something better be embodied by me, and may my healthy choices encourage with love my seven generations forward and back to make their own healthy choices for the highest healing good, harming none."

This list is burned at the full moon to harness its power to manifest.

To do a general healing for my ancestral line, I like to go to my ancestral altar, raise my hands to surround the altar, and visualize a ball of Reiki forming around the altar. In that ball I visualize my ancestral lines going back through time to the beginning. Then I do the distance symbol in my mind inside the ball and do a distance Reiki session. This can also be directed toward an inheritance pattern by setting the intention to heal a pattern. I usually finish with a prayer, something similar to the one in the written petition.

Reiki Candles

As a Witch, I was burning candles for healing long before I learned Reiki. It is one method of healing in my bag of tricks that has been effective for me more times than I can even count. When my friends ask, I will light a candle for them in their time of need. I use a Reiki candle when I don't have time for a full distance Reiki session or I think that the person needs a continuous flow of Reiki to alleviate a pressing disease. I keep a drawer stocked with a multitude of colored candles for this work. You can also use this method if you want to manifest or banish something.

As I have said before, I like to time my work with the moon: waxing to manifest and waning to banish. The one exception for me is healing work, because it is both. You can tailor your candle color to the moon tide if you like. A candle for a person with an abscessed tooth during the waxing moon could be white for all-around healing or blue for soothing infection, whereas in the waning moon, you would use purple for transformation, gray for neutralizing, or black for banishing. Aligning your working with the moon phase can add punch to it, but such timing is not necessary for an emergency healing.

I like to check the healing color table in Christopher Penczak's book *The Inner Temple of Witchcraft* (it's found on page 264) for suggestions for different diseases. He also has a pretty comprehensive color list for candle intentions in the appendix to his book *Magick of Reiki.* If you are in a pinch, white is the best color to have around because it contains all colors and can be used for any goal or healing. When in doubt, go with the healing color that speaks to you at the time. Trust your intuition to help you choose the right one for the situation. For healing an abscessed tooth, my intuition leads me to blue, where Christopher suggests purple or violet. I love Christopher, but you can bet good money I will go with my intuition because it sees more than my conscious mind can process.

In this case, I would take out my blue candle and get a metal holder for it. I like to carve Reiki symbols that align with what I am healing. Since this is a physical healing, I would use the empowerment symbol, and since it is at a distance, I would add the distance symbol. I might also add the emotional symbol because it may have roots in the emotions. There are other symbols you could incorporate, but I like the simple three. I will usually use a knife or nail to carve them in.

The next step is to anoint the candle in a healing oil or potion. My healing oil at the present comes from a Scott Cunningham formula of eucalyptus, orange, and pine essential oils mixed with a base of grapeseed oil (if you don't have these particular oils, you can use sunflower oil or olive oil). I like to move from the center of the candle outward toward the ends when banishing, and from the ends of the candle to the center for manifesting. Other traditions do it differently, but this is the method that has always stuck with me. After this is done, I Reiki the candle until I feel that it is charged. You should be able to feel when it is full. I like to say an intention prayer over the candle. This statement has changed over the years, but is based on writings of Silver Ravenwolf and Marion Weinstein. It goes like this:

"By the one power that is the Goddess and God

from which all Reiki and healing emanates,

Who work through me and with me

To bring about healing (or manifestation, clearing, or any intention)

I charge this candle to burn in service of the light

(here is where the intention comes in)

To heal Charley Chuckle's abscessed tooth

and to return him to perfect health on all levels.

I ask this for the highest healing good of all concerned and harming none.

So mote it be!"

Then I place and light the candle. I clap my hands three times to symbolize letting go of any attachment or cords created and let the candle do its work. I like to put mine either on my altar when I am near by or in our fireplace. Sometimes if I feel the situation is desperate, I will put the candle in the sink or bathtub to burn overnight. If you can't do this, it is perfectly fine to snuff your candles and relight them when you can watch them. I feel this makes the healing take a bit longer, though, so if it is an emergency, I let it burn through the night until it is done. When the healing is done, sometimes I will burn a white candle as an offering in gratitude for the healing.

Sending Reiki
Into the Future

Reiki is a powerful way to help heal our past. We can send the Reiki back, but we can also send it forward. Using your distance Reiki, you can charge a place, a time, or a person with Reiki. Sending Reiki into the future takes some planning ahead. To do this you should assess what your needs might be in the months to come.

An easy example would be that you have a surgery coming up, and you want to recover quickly. You know the date of your surgery and about what time it is scheduled to be done. You should have a plan of where you are going to recover from it and when. During your Reiki session, state the date, place, and person (in this case yourself). Use the distance symbol to connect through the oneness of all space and time in spirit. You may want to use a prayer of intention to focus your mind:

"I send this Reiki through time and space to Grand View Manor on Monday, January 5th, 2015 to Adam Sartwell for his highest healing good, harming none."

With this method, you can repeat your Reiki session multiple times to really charge up the day so the healing energy is strong and potent. You can also set it to take place over a longer time frame, like a week or a month. Just know that the broader you stretch the time frame, the less concentrated the Reiki across that time. If you are going to do a longer span, do more distance Reiki sessions during the week or month beforehand to send enough healing energy to be effective.

This can also be used to charge days that you feel you might need a little extra energy or just want everything to go for the highest good: during a job interview, on a first date, giving divorce papers, having your day in court, attending a spiritual retreat, or any other high intensity day. You can even set an intention when you start to charge that day, focusing on what you would like to manifest. Just remember that with Reiki, the results will be for the highest healing good for all involved and you may not get what you intended completely to the letter—or it may go better than you imagined!

Cleansing Your Home

Our homes hold energy just like our bodies do. Imagine every fight you've ever had and every long day at work that you've brought home lingering in the corners of every room. Now imagine this has happened since the construction of your home to everyone who has ever lived in it. If you live in a newly built home, you may not have to deal with energies of former owners, just contractors and other workers. But if you're like me and live in a house that was built in 1898, there might be a lot of residual energies lurking about.

We also fill our homes with our stuff. Our possessions and where we place them affect the flow of energy in the home. Over time this can create a toxic environment for those who live or pass through there, affecting our health and our energetic being. Reiki can help you cleanse your home's energy bodies.

The first step is to physically clean your home. Clear away the clutter. Recycle it, throw it out, or give it away. Ask yourself if you have used the things in your home in the last year and whether you realistically see yourself using them in the future. When we clear away these things, we make room for new blessings.

Clean away the dust that has been building up. Vacuum or sweep the floors. Once you feel like you have tidied up, it is time to cleanse the energies of the house. Get yourself some salt, water, and a stick of incense aligned with cleansing like sage, lavender, or frankincense and myrrh. Mix the salt and water in a bowl and Reiki them to charge them for cleansing. Reiki charge your incense stick before lighting it for cleansing as well.

Go from room to room with these implements. Lightly sprinkle some of the salt water. Take your burning incense and draw the empowerment symbol in the four directions of the room. Walk the room as if you were making a big empowerment symbol with your movements in the room while holding out the incense. At this point I like to imagine the violet flame that burns away all that doesn't serve, transforming its energies, or visualize the room filled with water that is draining away, leaving it clean and fresh.

When this step is done, draw an emotional symbol in the middle of the room and over any of the doors where people would enter. Draw the empowerment symbol over any windows or openings. The emotional symbol acts like a screen to neutralize any emotional energy lingering on a person when they go through the door. The empowerment symbol brings protection to other openings and cleanses the area. When you feel a room has been cleansed, move to the next one and repeat the process until every room in your home is cleansed. Don't forget closets and basements!

When you have moved through the whole place, draw the empowerment symbol for protection over the doors to the outside. Then draw the emotional symbol to help filter out any unwanted emotional energies people might bring in with them. You may want to sit in the space and do a Reiki charging of the home using the distance method, visualizing the place between your hands and giving it Reiki until you feel done. A prayer of blessing of your choosing is a great closing to "seal" the whole process.

Body Checking
and Spot Reiki

Our body is deeply connected to the subconscious mind. They are intrinsically intertwined. Our subconscious stores memories, reactions, emotions, stress, and complexes in the body. It is part of its job to hold on to these things. We sometimes tell it to do so by focusing our energy on certain things through our conscious mind. Sometimes it is just something that naturally upsets or triggers us. These stored energies can become illness if given time to gather strength. One way to help prevent this is to do a body check-in and then spot Reiki.

You will need about fifteen to twenty minutes to do this. It can be done in the morning when you wake up, before bed, or maybe on your lunch break at work, basically whenever you can take time to relax for fifteen minutes.

Begin by taking a few deep breaths. Imagine waves of relaxation beginning to flow down from the crown of your head. Relax your scalp and the muscles around your eyes. Relax your jaw and your neck. Release any tension in your shoulders and your arms. Let the waves of relaxation flow down into your chest and upper back. Relax your belly and your lower back. Release any tension in your buttocks and thighs. Relax your knees and your calves. Let the waves of relaxation gently flow through your body, pushing any tension out the bottom of your feet into Mother Earth for recycling.

After you have relaxed your body, ask it to show you any zones where you have a block to be released. Gently do a sweep of your body just like you did with releasing tension, working from crown to feet. A packet of energy may feel like a small pain, a place of tension, a tingly area, a cold or hot spot, or you may have your own signal. Really focus on what your body is telling you. Once you have found that spot, imagine your consciousness moving from your head to that spot. Ask your body/subconscious to show you the root of this block. After you ask the question, clear your mind and wait for the answer. For me it is usually the first thing I have pop into my mind. It may be a memory, a picture, a feeling, a color, a sound, or any way your subconscious likes to communicate.

After you have experienced its root, ask your body if it is ready to let it go. You will get a feeling of yes or no. If no, thank your body for showing that to you and ask it if there is another spot you can work on today and repeat the process. If yes, begin to Reiki that spot and allow your body to help you remove that block. Sometimes if the problem is really persistent, you may need to remove that energy from your body. Call to your guides to come and help you remove the blockage. You may feel hands on you pulling the blockage gently out and releasing it to be recycled. Reiki the spot until the Reiki stops flowing. Then gently sweep the energy of the spot in a smoothing gesture to stabilize it.

From here you could move to the next zone of tension if you have time, repeating the steps of asking, listening, asking, Reiki, and smoothing. When you are done, thank your body for showing you these blockages. Then bring your focus back to your head. Gently move your extremities to bring you back into waking consciousness. You may want to sweep the aura to ground yourself. I will sometimes tap my body with my fingers to bring myself back to waking consciousness if I feel like I am not fully back.

Reiki for Family, Friends & Adversaries

I once had this meditation tape from the Edgar Cayce Foundation that I bought from a used book store when I was in high school. I used it in my psychology class in high school when I presented meditation to the class. It was your basic "relax, focus on your breath, begin to breathe in white light" meditation. Towards the end of the meditation, you would ground out the energy by sending that white light to a close friend or family member, an acquaintance, and to someone who was an adversary or enemy, the principle being that by doing so, you would both prevent overloading yourself with energy and also make the world a better place.

The meditation also suggested that if some intuition came to you about any of the people you'd sent light to, you should share it with them. Depending on their spiritual beliefs, you could share the origins of the intuition or just say you dreamed it, but regardless, you should always ask them if they wanted to hear it first. That trilogy of family-friend-adversary has always stuck with me because it is a great example of giving away energy that eases our karma in this world. I think this is also a great Reiki practice and can have marvelous results.

Ethically, I think it is a breach to send Reiki or energy to people who are unaware. If the person doesn't seem open to Reiki or energy work, I usually ask the person if I can pray for them. Asking is not always an option with everyone, however, especially an adversary. To solve this issue, I usually call on the higher selves of both myself and the person I want to Reiki, asking the higher selves if it is okay. You can use muscle testing or a pendulum if you are unsure of your ability to be clear and objective with whatever answer might intuitively come.

Cyndi Dale uses this method of connecting to the higher selves of her clients and calls it Spirit to Spirit. It is usually done with a prayer asking your higher self to be present and then asking the higher self of the other person to be present, and then asking them to talk and facilitate healing. She uses this method to solve problems between people as well. Christopher Penczak has a similar exercise in his book, *The Temple of Shamanic Witchcraft*.

To do this distance healing for a family, friend, and adversary, first call on your higher self with a prayer such as the following:

"In the name of the infinite source from which all Reiki flows, I ask for my higher self, my Bornless One, my Watcher, the part of my being that holds my truest Will, my unconditional compassion, and my deepest wisdom, to be present with me to guide this work and facilitate communication with the higher selves of those I wish to heal. I thank my highest self and the infinite source for this aid and all favors. So mote it be!"

Then connect to the higher self of the person you are going to work on:

"I ask that Hester Prim's higher self commune with my higher self as I ask if would it be acceptable for me to send Reiki to them now."

You will either get a feeling of yes or no within seconds. If you don't—or if you aren't sure—use muscle testing or a pendulum to check in. When you get a yes, send the Reiki like you normally would doing a distance Reiki session. Repeat this for the two others on your list of family, friend, and adversary.

You can also do this model of sending Reiki to people more intuitively by calling on your higher self as before, then asking your higher self to guide you to the person who is willing to accept Reiki and has a need within your family and close friends, your acquaintances, and your adversaries, one category at a time. For me I usually get a picture in my mind of the person. You may receive a feeling of a person, "hear" their name, or just know who to send it to. If you are doing this method, you already know that it is going to be accepted.

This healing method has helped me be closer with family and friends. It has also smoothed the way to forgiveness for my adversaries and to a realization of what shadow part of myself is reflected in them. If you want, you could also add a situation you want to heal to the list of family-friend-adversary. Using the intuitive method with a situation can be surprising because situations you didn't know were problematic will pop up. This is a great way to share the wealth of Reiki and to act locally to heal the world.

Psychic Senses &
Scanning Energy Bodies

When you are scanning yourself or another person, you will find that, depending on your psychic ability, you may become aware of places in the energy body where the energy is different. You may feel cold, heat, aches, phantom pains, tingling, or motion. These are the usual responses for psychic feeling or clairsentence. Psychic feeling is the most common psychic response because Reiki is based on touch or feeling. Each one of these can tell you something about what is going on in the person's energy body, although please note that there may be differences between people because our feelings are processed through our subconscious and everyone's is a bit different.

What I have observed is that cold spots are holes in the aura. These holes can happen for multiple reasons. They can be caused by outside influences or by the person's own emotional responses. These holes are openings where unwanted energies or thought-forms can enter, so note any you sense when doing a scanning and go back to this place to fill it in with Reiki. Often when my hands feel cold to me, the person on the table will report that in that spot, my hands felt hot or burning. This is not always the case, because not everyone is aware of or feels things in the same way.

Heat or hot spots are usually thought-forms to me. These thought-forms are packets of energy in the aura that have a pattern created by thoughts and emotions. These do not always belong to the person you are healing. They may be someone else's that have been impressed upon them. If this is the case, an aura hole usually accompanies them. There are two ways to deal with this. One is to keep the Reiki on the thought-form until it begins to dissolve under the healing flow. The other is to do a psychic surgery where you or a trusted guide completely remove the energy packet and fill in the space with Reiki. Both work, but the first technique lets the energy get recycled by the aura and go to a different purpose. If the energy feels different from the person you are working on and is accompanied by a hole, scooping it out and replacing it with Reiki is a better option because the energy's origin was outside the body, which might not be able to process it.

Tingling or motion are my psychic tells that a cord is present. Each of us makes cords in our aura to those whom we are connected. This can be through love, hate, and any emotion in between. Usually if I sense a cord, it is because it no longer serves the person. There are the rare cases where I feel in my gut not to remove a cord, but make the person aware it is there. Sometimes these cords serve a purpose. To remove the cord, I like to grab it with my hand and give it a shake. I ask if the person can feel anything I am doing. Usually they feel a tugging. I then remove the cord and ask my healing guide to take the end somewhere safe to dispose of it. Then I Reiki the spot where the cord was attached.

Aches or phantom pains in your own body are caused by sympathetic empathy. Sometimes you can get a lot of information as to the state of your client just from observing your own body for places of stress or pain. When these come up for me, I thank my body and my guides for the message, and usually it will fade. After the session, when I tell the client about the phantom pain, I usually learn that they have suffered a past injury in that spot.

These are common clairsentient feelings for body scanning. They don't include some of the other intuitive ways you can sense these issues. While working on one of my first scans, I told my teacher I saw colors in different parts of the body, which is a part of my natural clairvoyance. I have experienced words and instructions while working on clients. Sometimes I will even have a knowing about why and how an injury happened. Some clients like when you share your insights, and some just want to have a relaxing silent Reiki session. I usually leave it up to them because I feel that reading a person who doesn't want to be read is unethical. Go with the flow of what the client says they need. You can tell them after it is done what you felt during the session, if they want to hear it.

The Empowerment Symbol

The Reiki symbols don't just just give us a connection to deeper healing powers; they can also open us to different levels of reality when we are meditating. Our journey work with the Reiki symbols can help us to learn more about ourselves and get guidance from the other realm. The following is a meditation that can be used with the empowerment symbol to enter your personal Reiki healing temple. Your healing temple is your own space on the planes where you can control what is going on, get healing from your guides, and interact with your higher guidance.

Get yourself ready to meditate by getting comfortable and making sure you won't be disturbed. Imagine waves of relaxation flowing from your head down to your toes. Focus your attention on each muscle group as you relax. Let any tension flow out of your toes into Mother Earth to be recycled. Relax your mind and imagine all your thoughts are clouds being blown away by a gentle breeze. When you have a clear blue sky in your imagination, relax your heart, letting any emotions or stresses flow away. Let the light within your heart and your spirit protect and guide you.

Now we are going to count down into a meditative state by counting down from 12 to 1 and imagining it on the screen of our mind. Bring up on the screen of your mind the number 12. You can draw it or just imagine it appearing like a movie screen. Now it fades, and you write 11 on the screen of your mind. Draw 10 on the screen of your mind. Getting more relaxed with each number. Draw 9 on the screen. Draw 8 on your screen. Draw 7 on your screen. Draw 6 on your screen. Feeling a deepening relaxation. Draw 5 on your screen. Draw 4. Draw 3. Draw 2 on the screen. Draw 1. You are now in a meditative state where all you do is for the highest good.

Release your screen and count down from 13 to 1 just listening to the numbers and going deeper with each one: 13, 12 ,11, 10, 9, 8, 7, 6, 5, 4, 3, 2, 1. You are now in a journey state and ready to safely explore.

On the screen of your mind, visualize a door. This is a special door that goes to your own personal healing temple. This healing temple's door has the empowerment symbol of Reiki carved into it. To open the door, you have to trace the symbol. As you do so, you leave a trail of light that makes the symbol glow. The door opens for you. As you step through, you come into your own personal healing temple.

As you explore your temple, know that each experience of a healing temple is different. You may find that you have a guide in your temple waiting for you. Greet your guide and get to know them. After you have spoken for a while, ask them if they have any information that you need to know right now. Know that since they are in your healing temple, they are there to keep you in perfect health.

When you are ready to conclude your time in your temple, give thanks to your guide. Return to the door. As you step through the door, it closes behind you. The symbol fades. Step back into your body as your door fades from your mind's eye.

Begin to count yourself up to a waking consciousness by counting 1 to 13: 1, 2, 3, 4, 5, 6, 7, 8, 9, 10, 11, 12, 13. Begin to wiggle your toes and hands as you begin to come fully back. Count yourself up again from 1 to 12, coming back more fully into your body with each number: 1, 2, 3, 4, 5, 6, 7, 8, 9, 10, 11, 12. You are now fully awake and refreshed.

Know that you can return at any time to receive healing and guidance from your guides. This is your own spiritual place of healing and power.

The Mental-Emotional Symbol

The second journey through the Reiki symbols is through the emotional-mental symbol. This symbol transports us to the mental and emotional plane, where we can communicate with our unconscious mind and the minds of others. This is also the place where all the knowledge of the world is collected; some call this the Akashic Records. This is the place where karma, patterns, and past lives are all stored. It is where forgiveness can happen, where you can discover the reasons behind your experiences.

To begin this journey, get comfortable and make sure that you won't be disturbed. Imagine waves of relaxation flowing from your head down to your toes. Focus your attention on each muscle group as you relax. Let any tension flow out of your toes into Mother Earth to be recycled. Relax your mind, and imagine all your thoughts are clouds being blown away by a gentle breeze. When you have a clear blue sky in your imagination, relax your heart, letting any emotions or stresses flow away. Let the light within your heart and your spirit protect and guide you.

Now you are going to count down into a meditative state by counting down from 12 to 1, imagining it on the screen of your mind. Bring up the number 12 on the screen of your mind. You can draw it, or just imagine it appearing like on a movie screen. Now it fades, and you write 11 on the screen of your mind. Draw 10 on the screen of your mind. Getting more relaxed with each number. Draw 9 on the screen. Draw 8 on your screen. Draw 7 on your screen. Draw 6 on your screen. Feeling a deepening relaxation. Draw 5 on your screen. Draw 4. Draw 3. Draw 2 on the screen. Draw 1. You are now in a meditative state where all you do is for the highest good.

Release your screen and count down from 13 to 1 just listening to the numbers and going deeper. 13, 12 ,11, 10, 9, 8, 7, 6, 5, 4, 3, 2, 1. You are now in a journey state and ready to safely explore.

Conjure the door with the emotional-mental symbol on it. See it and feel its solidity. Trace the symbol on the door, visualizing your tracing of it, lighting up the symbol. This is the key to opening the door. Walk through the door into your own interpretation of the Akashic Records. It may be a large library, a crystal cave, or something of your own making. Within your Akashic Records, you have a way of interfacing with information, items such as books, crystals, computers, or something of your own design.

Think of an issue you are dealing with. You will be guided to the section that deals with this issue. Read the records to discover the higher purpose of this issue and any information you need. If you can't find the information you need, know that there are guides to this place able to help you.

Once you have found the reasons for the issue, you can make better decisions, because sometimes just knowing the reason for a problem can get you to the heart of its lesson and it will fade from your life. Thank the hall of records and return to the door. As you come out of your door, it closes behind you. The symbol fades. Step back into your body, and your door fades from your mind's eye.

Begin to count yourself up to a waking consciousness by first counting 1 to 13: 1, 2, 3, 4, 5, 6, 7, 8, 9, 10, 11, 12, 13. Begin to wiggle your toes and hands as you begin to come fully back. Count yourself up again from 1 to 12 coming more back into your body with each number: 1, 2, 3, 4, 5, 6, 7, 8, 9, 10, 11, 12. You are now fully awake and refreshed.

The Distance Symbol

The third doorway journey is through the distance symbol—the symbol that connects us to the spiritual level where all time and space dissolve into one. This is why we can Reiki past events to heal them in the present or send Reiki into the future to charge a day. This is how we can send Reiki to people thousands of miles away. This is the symbol that opens the way to time and space travel on the planes. You can use it to go to past lives. You can use it to go see what next week is like. You can use it to give Reiki to someone while you are astral projecting to them. You can use it for any journey of healing. Choose a destination before you begin this meditation. It doesn't provide a lot of detail in the middle because you will have an experience of traveling to your destination, and it will be unique for everyone.

Turn off the phone, get comfortable, and make sure you won't be disturbed. Imagine waves of relaxation flowing from your head down to your toes. Focus your attention on each muscle group as you relax. Let any tension flow out of your toes into Mother Earth to be recycled. Relax your mind, and imagine all your thoughts are clouds being blown away by a gentle breeze. When you have a clear blue sky in your imagination, relax your heart, letting any emotions or stresses flow away. Let the light within your heart and your spirit protect and guide you.

Now we are going to count down into a meditative state by first counting down from 12 to 1 and imagining it on the screen of our mind. Bring up the number 12 on the screen of your mind. You can draw it or just imagine it appearing like on a movie screen. Now it fades, and you write 11 on the screen of your mind. Draw 10 on the screen of your mind. Getting more relaxed with each number. Draw 9 on the screen. Draw 8 on your screen. Draw 7 on your screen. Draw 6 on your screen. Feeling a deepening relaxation. Draw 5 on your screen. Draw 4. Draw 3. Draw 2 on the screen. Draw 1. You are now in a meditative state where all you do is for the highest good.

Release your screen and count down from 13 to 1 just listening to the numbers and going deeper: 13, 12 ,11, 10, 9, 8, 7, 6, 5, 4, 3, 2, 1. You are now in a journey state and ready to safely explore.

Visualize a door on the screen of your mind. This is a special door that goes to the destination you wish to visit. You will see that it has the distance symbol carved into its wood. Set your intention of where in time and space you wish to go. Trace the distance symbol on the door. It lights up as you begin to trace the symbol. The door opens, and you step through. Observe your destination. What does it feel like? What does it look like? Explore.

When you feel like you have gotten what you need from this destination, return to your door. As you come out of your door, it closes behind you. The symbol fades. Step back into your body, and your door fades from your mind's eye.

Begin to count yourself up to waking consciousness by counting first 1 to 13: 1, 2, 3, 4, 5, 6, 7, 8, 9, 10, 11, 12, 13. Begin to wiggle your toes and hands as you begin to come fully back. Count yourself up again from 1 to 12, returning more fully into your body with each number: 1, 2, 3, 4, 5, 6, 7, 8, 9, 10, 11, 12. You are now fully awake and refreshed.

You can use this meditation to go anywhere in time and space. You can also heal things in different times and places by going there and doing the healing yourself instead of sending the energy of Reiki to do it for you.

Crystal Balls as Surrogates

The crystal ball has become a symbol synonymous with fortune telling. We have all seen the pictures of the woman with a head scarf gazing into her crystal ball, passing her hand over it mystically. Using a crystal ball to get information and guidance is an art in and of itself. Since this is a book about Reiki, we are going to talk about how a crystal ball makes not only a great Reiki surrogate for distance Reiki, but also a great hands-on healer.

There are multiple kinds of crystal balls out there on the market. The lead glass ones are not the ones I am talking about for healing. (Though one of my favorite scrying devices is a lead crystal ball inherited from Christopher's mother, I don't use it in healing, and I am pretty sure she didn't either.) I am talking about crystal balls made from actual stones and minerals from the earth. My favorite healing crystal ball is a clear quartz.

The benefits of using a healing crystal ball for your distance Reiki is that it naturally amplifies your healing Reiki. Quartz has been used for years to enhance the energy in our energy bodies and improve our resonance. When you use a crystal ball to do distance Reiki, you can also incorporate the "sight" to get readings on what your patient needs most. You can also use it to get guidance from their higher self. Using a crystal ball for Reiki also charges up the ball, allowing you to place it in the area where healing will be enhanced.

To use a crystal ball as a surrogate, first cleanse the ball with running water, smudging, visualization of violet flame, or by letting it sit in some salt. Take the crystal ball and hold it in your hands. Draw the empowerment symbol over the ball. Then draw the emotional symbol over the ball. Then lastly draw the distance symbol over the ball and state the intention of where you want the healing to go.

After you have said this, hold the ball between your hands, giving it Reiki. Let your focus go soft. Breathe deeply. You may notice shapes or symbols in the crystal. Know that this is your unconscious giving you messages in symbolic language about the state of the person or the healing. Gently ask your unconscious to show you the person being healed. If they don't psychically appear to you, imagine seeing them in the crystal ball. Close your eyes if it helps you get in touch with the picture. Continue to let the Reiki flow. One of the methods I like to use is to visualize the ball focusing on the chakras one at a time to clear and cleanse them during the healing. The ball may get really hot in you hands. This is okay; just continue until you feel that it is time to stop.

When you feel that the healing is done, repeat your intention of healing for this person's highest good and return the crystal ball to its holder. Draw Raku over the ball, and then clap your hands three times to separate from the healing.

I use quartz for these healings because of its natural ability to amplify. You could also use amethyst or experiment with other crystal balls. Christopher's mother, Rosalie, loved using crystal balls for healing and would charge them up and give them to people to meditate with. The ambient healing that flows from a charged ball can give great healing over time. If you are a Reiki master, you may want to attune your crystal ball to Reiki to give it an extra punch. I invite you to experiment on your own to find the ball that works best for you.

The Healing Reiki Circle

Since I am both a Witch and a Reiki Master, the combination of the occult magick circle and the healing power of Reiki seems like a natural progression, blending two harmonious paths. I love to do this during my healing rituals for the Temple of Witchcraft, using a Reiki circle to create a sacred space and time for burning petitions of healing, the Temple's healing list, and my own goal lists. It makes the act of releasing the healing so much more powerful and focused. I know not everyone wants to blend Reiki with their witchcraft or vice versa, and that is okay. For me, though, it is a ritual of power and healing. I have written the following ritual to use at the new moon when I release the Temple's healing to those on the healing list.

To do the ritual, you are going to need some things: a cauldron or pot for burning your petitions in, the petitions themselves, a lighter or matches, and an altar that it is safe to burn on. I usually do this ritual outside. Some optional things you can add to the ritual include incense for healing, charged candles, crystals, or any other healing accoutrements.

Set your altar. I like to have the cauldron with the petitions in the middle of the altar. Begin by facing north. Put out your dominant hand and imagine a healing flow of Reiki that shoots out like a beam, making a ring around you as you walk around the space of your circle. Do three circuits around the circle visualizing this ring. I like to set my intention with these words:

"I cast this circle of Reiki to protect the healing work I am about to do. I charge it to draw in healing power and to disperse any energies that are harmful. I consecrate it to be a space beyond space, a time beyond time, where the highest healing good reigns supreme. So mote it be!"

I clap my hands to cut off the flow and seal the circle. Then facing the north, I call to the healers of the elements around the circle:

"To the north I call to the healers of earth, healers of the body, and healers of the land, be with me in this circle to lend me your wisdom and your power. Hail and welcome."

Face the east and say:

"To the east I call to the healers of fire, healers of the spirit, and healers of energy, be with me in this circle and lend me your wisdom and your power. Hail and welcome."

Face the south and say:

"To the south I call to the healers of air, healers of the mind, and keepers of healing knowledge, be with me in this circle and lend me your wisdom and your power. Hail and welcome."

Face the west and say:

"To the west I call to the healers of water, healers of emotion, and healers of the past. Be with me in this circle and lend me your wisdom and your power. Hail and welcome."

Go to the altar. We have created a sacred space around us, and now it is time to bring divine energy into the circle. For this invocation, you may want to have a charged white candle or other candle of your choice to represent the deity you want to invoke. I invite you to come up with one of your own invocations to your healing deity. Here is a generic one that calls on the Great Spirit:

"I call to the infinite source from which all Reiki flows. Great Spirit in all your healing guises, be with me in this space. Guide this healing work. Bless my circle with your divine presence. Blessed be."

I also call to the Reiki Masters beyond the veil to be with me. I like to make this one up on the fly. I encourage you to come up with your own prayer to them and for them.

I then draw the Reiki symbols over the cauldron with the petitions in it. I give them some more Reiki just before I burn them. I like to set the intention with some words of power before I light them. You can use mine or something of your own:

"By the infinite source from which all Reiki comes, I ask that all requests for healing, banishing, and manifestation within this cauldron manifest for the highest healing good, harming none. I thank the infinite for all my blessings and for this healing work. So mote it be!"

Then I light the petitions and let them burn down. When they have turned to ash, I will put the lid on the cauldron to let them snuff and cool.

I then thank the infinite for its presence in my own words. I thank the Reiki Masters in the same manner.

Then turning to the north, I release the healers:

"I give thanks to the healers of earth, the healers of the body and the land. Go forth with my blessing. Hail and farewell."

Then turn to the west:

"I give thanks to the healers of water, the healers of emotion and of the past. Go forth with my blessing. Hail and farewell."

Facing the south:

"I give thanks to the healers of air, healers of thought and keepers of knowledge. Go forth with my blessing. Hail and farewell."

Facing the east:

"I give thanks to the healers of fire, healers of spirit and of energy. Go forth with my blessing. Hail and farewell.

Then I walk the circle counterclockwise imagining it expanding out as a wave of healing saying:

"I cast this circle out into the cosmos as a healing wave of energy; may those in need of its healing receive it for their highest healing good, harming none. So mote it be!"

The ritual is done. Dispose of the ashes responsibly.

About the Author

Adam Sartwell is a Reiki Master Teacher. He has practiced witchcraft for 21 years and counting. He is an accomplished psychic reader and healer. He and his two partners co-founded the Temple of Witchcraft, a religious non-profit where he is Virgo lead minister in charge of the healing ministries, and he helped to found Copper Cauldron Publishing. Find out more at *templeofwitchcraft.org* and *coppercauldronpublishing.com*.

www.ingramcontent.com/pod-product-compliance
Lightning Source LLC
Chambersburg PA
CBHW071634040426
42452CB00009B/1623